LAW AND MORALS

LAW
AND MORALS

CARDINAL CAHAL B. DALY

FOUR COURTS PRESS

This book was typeset by
Gilbert Gough Typesetting for
Four Courts Press Ltd.
Kill Lane, Blackrock, Co. Dublin

© Cahal B. Daly 1993

A catalogue record for this title
is available from the British Library.

ISBN 1-85182-119-8

Printed in Ireland
by Colour Books Ltd, Dublin.

CONTENTS

Preface   7

Morality and Law   9

Morality and Being Human   45

PREFACE

The question of the relationship between morals and law is a perennial one. It has been associated in more recent times with the celebrated debate between the late Lord Devlin and Professor H.L.A. Hart. It takes on new actuality in Ireland in the light of recent and current debates on such grave issues as abortion and divorce. While not entering directly into the detail of these debates, the present short work attempts to set them in the wider context of contemporary philosophical and legal discussion and to point to some of the major moral and ethical questions underlying the debates.

The first paper, "Morality and Law", has not been published before. The second, "Morality and Being Human", is a revised version of a text which first appeared in the book, *Philosophy and Totality*, published by the Department of Scholastic Philosophy, the Queen's University of Belfast, in 1977. The text was then entitled, "Ethics and the Whole Man". It is republished here, with amendments and additions, by kind permission of that Department and the University.

These papers will be found deficient in such scholarly apparatus as bibliographical references, footnotes, et cetera. A bishop's life, unfortunately, does not leave time for such accompaniments of scholarship. I can only apologise for their absence.

My sincere thanks are offered to Mrs Frances Doran, who typed the material, and to Mr Michael Adams, of Four

Courts Press, for much patience, advice and help in seeing the text through to publication.

MORALITY AND LAW

The question is much debated as to whether it is the law's function to protect the morality of society, and therefore, if not to make people virtuous, at least in some sense to keep them so; or whether the law should be concerned exclusively with the prevention of actions which cause harm to others. The contrast between the two conceptions of law is clearly expressed in two quotations, one from the late Lord Devlin and the other from Professor H.L.A. Hart. Lord Devlin wrote:

> The true principle is that the law exists for the protection of society. It does not discharge its function by protecting the individual from injury, annoyance, corruption, and exploitation; the law must protect also the institutions and the community of ideas, political and moral, without which people cannot live together. Society cannot ignore the morality of the individual any more than it can his loyalty; it flourishes on both and without either it dies.[1]

Professor H.L.A. Hart devoted his Harry Camp Lectures at Stanford University in 1962 to the criticism of the view which he characterises thus:

> It is the view that the criminal law may properly be

1. "Morals and the Criminal Law", the celebrated Maccabaean Lecture of 1959, reprinted in *The Enforcement of Morals* (Oxford, 1965), 22.

used to punish immorality as such, even if it causes no harm to others.[2]

THE HERITAGE OF MILL

The dispute is, of course, an old and regularly recurring one in the history of the philosophy of morals and the philosophy of law. The debate between Hart and Devlin in recent times is really not substantially different from the debate between John Stuart Mill and James Fitzjames Stephen in the last century. Stephen's contention that the law "may and can protect an acknowledged moral standard", was directed against John Stuart Mill's essay, *On Liberty*. Professor Hart freely and frequently acknowledges his indebtedness to Mill. Indeed, he contends that it is a weakness of English law that it has not an adequately developed philosophy of law; and this in turn is due to the fact that "the philosophy which has dominated English thought about law", namely the philosophy of Jeremy Bentham and John Stuart Mill, "has scarcely ever been shared by the few English judges who have articulated general views about law." Hart's own philosophy of law is substantially the same as that of Mill. In the matter concerning us in the present chapter, this philosophy is expressed in Mill's famous paragraph:

> The object of this Essay is to assert one very simple principle, as entitled to govern absolutely the dealings of society with the individual in the way of compulsion and control, whether the means used be physical force in the form of legal penalties, or the moral coercion of public opinion. That principle is, that the sole end for which mankind are warranted, individually or collect-

2. *Law, Liberty and Morality*, Oxford, 1963, Preface.

ively, in interfering with the liberty of action of any of their number, is self-protection. That the only purpose for which power can be rightfully exercised over any member of a civilised community, against his will, is to prevent harm to others. His own good, either physical or moral, is not a sufficient warrant. . . . To justify (compelling or punishing a man), the conduct from which it is desired to deter him must be calculated to produce evil to someone else. The only part of the conduct of anyone, for which he is amenable to society, is that which concerns others. In the part which merely concerns himself, his independence is, of right, absolute.[3]

WOLFENDEN AND AFTER

This thinking of Mill has become part of the bloodstream of English liberalism. Like the circulation of the blood, its operation is largely unconscious. If it "rushes to the head", it may do this much rather as passion and impassioned utterance than as reasoned and critically evaluated thought. Mill's statement is, for example, a dominant influence on the reasoning and the recommendations of the English Committee on Homosexual Offences and Prostitution, otherwise known as the Wolfenden Committee, as we find these in its Report, presented in 1957. The echoes of the essay *On Liberty* are unmistakable in the following paragraphs:

> We clearly recognise that the laws of any society must be acceptable to the general moral sense of the community if they are to be respected and enforced. But

3. *On Liberty* (Everyman edition, London, 1948), 72-3.

we are not charged to enter into matters of private moral conduct except in-so-far as they directly affect the public good. . . .[4]

It is not, in our view, the function of the law to intervene in the private lives of citizens, or to seek to enforce any particular pattern of behaviour. . . .[5]

There remains one additional counter-argument which we believe to be decisive, namely the importance which society and the law ought to give to individual freedom of choice and action in matters of private morality. Unless a deliberate attempt is to be made by society, acting through the agency of the law, to equate the sphere of crime with that of sin, there must remain a realm of private morality and immorality which is, in brief and crude terms, not the law's business. To say this is not to condone or encourage private immorality. On the contrary, to emphasise the personal and private nature of moral or immoral conduct is to emphasise the personal and private responsibility of the individual for his own actions, and that is a responsibility which a mature agent can properly be expected to carry for himself without the threat of punishment from the law.[6]

This is the essential justification given for the Committee's conclusion:

> We accordingly recommend that homosexual behaviour between consenting adults in private should no longer be a criminal offence.[7]

4. *Wolfenden Report*, 12. 5. Ibid., 14.
6. Ibid., 61. 7. Ibid., 62.

The same thinking pervades the second part of the Wolfenden Committee's Report, that concerned with the law and prostitution. It becomes clear at this point that Wolfenden was not the first Englishman to be brought up on a philosophical diet of undiluted Mill.

> The criminal law, as the Street Offences Committee plainly pointed out, "is not concerned with private morals or with ethical sanctions". This does not mean that society itself can be indifferent to these matters, for prostitution is an evil of which any society which claims to be civilised should seek to rid itself. . . . But until education and the moral sense of the community bring about a change of attitude towards the fact of prostitution, the law by itself cannot do so.[8]

> At the same time, the law has its place and function in this matter. We cannot do better than quote the words of the Street Offences committee:—"As a general proposition it will be universally accepted that the law is not concerned with private morals or with ethical sanctions. On the other hand, the law is plainly concerned with the outward conduct of citizens insofar as that conduct injures the rights of other citizens.[9]

This Wolfenden Report provides a direct link between Mill and the Devlin-Hart controversy, since Devlin's Maccabaean Lecture, "Morals and the Criminal Law", which originated this controversy, was devoted precisely to the critique of Wolfenden.

---

8. Ibid., 226. 9. Ibid., 229.

THE PHILOSOPHICAL FALLACIES OF UTILITARIANISM

It seems to me quite remarkable that Mill's views about law should be so readily assimilated without a critical evaluation of the ethical philosophy of Utilitarianism, from which his views on law, like his views on morality and on human society, derive. I do not profess here to provide such a philosophical critique. Suffice it to say that utilitarianism has, during and since Mill's time, been lashed by some of the most incisive minds and sharpest tongues in British philosophy, including the redoubtable F.H. Bradley and the formidable G.E. Moore. With Moore's refutation of Utilitarianism, as based on the "naturalistic fallacy", I deal below. I believe that it can fairly be regarded as one of the few examples of decisive and conclusive argument in the modern history of philosophy. As for Bradley, I can only let him speak for himself, since I cannot emulate his rhetoric and would not wish to imitate his rudeness:

> Hedonism *is* bankrupt; with weariness we have pursued it, through its various shapes, from the selfish doctrine of the individual to the self-sacrificing spirit of modern Utilitarianism. We have seen ... that in no shape will it give us a creed that holds water. ... Whatever we may think of those who embrace the doctrine, whatever may be its practical results, yet theoretically considered we have seen, I trust, that it is immoral and false. ... [10]

What is more to my present point is that there is a strange inconsistency in Mill's reasoning in the precise matter of law and morality. In his book, *Utilitarianism*, Mill claims to give

---

10. *Ethical Studies* (Oxford, 1927), 124.

us an objective and demonstrable, and indeed demonstrated, criterion of morality. He states it thus:

> The creed which accepts as the foundation of morals, Utility, or the Greatest Happiness Principle, holds that actions are right in proportion as they tend to promote happiness, wrong as they tend to produce the reverse of happiness. By happiness is intended pleasure, and the absence of pain; by unhappiness, pain and the privation of pleasure.[11]

It is strange that Mill did not himself see what was to be later made so blindingly clear by critics such as Bradley and Moore, that every single significant term in his proposition is ambiguous. "Happiness", "pleasure", "unhappiness", "pain"—each single one of these terms can be understood as connoting material/physical/psychological happiness, pleasure, etc. or moral happiness/unhappiness, moral pleasure/pain, spiritual satisfaction/spiritual discontent etc.

Moore cites Mills' celebrated argument, from *Utilitarianism*:

> The only proof capable of being given that a thing is visible is that people actually see it. The only proof that a sound as audible is that people hear it; and so of the other sources of our experience. In like manner, I apprehend, the sole evidence it is possible to produce that anything is desirable, is that people do actually desire it. . . . No reason can be given why the general happiness is desirable, except that each person, so far as he believes it to be attainable, desires his own happiness.[12]

11. *Utilitarianism* (Everyman edition, London, 1948), 6.
12. Ibid., 32-3.

Moore's devastating comment is the following:

> There, that is enough. That is my first point. Mill has made as naive and artless a use of the naturalistic fallacy as anybody could desire. "Good", he tells us, means "desirable", and you can only find out what is desirable by seeking to find out what is actually desired. . . .
>
> Well, the fallacy in this step is so obvious, that it is quite wonderful how Mill failed to see it. The fact is that "desirable" does not mean "able to be desired" as "visible" means "able to be seen". The desirable means simply what ought to be desired or deserves to be desired; just as the detestable means not what can be but what ought to be detested and the damnable what deserves to be damned. Mill has, then, smuggled in, under cover of the word "desirable" the very notion about which he ought to be quite clear. . . .[13]
>
> Mill tells us that we ought to desire something (an ethical proposition), because we actually do desire it; but if his contention that "I ought to desire" means nothing but "I do desire" were true, then he is only entitled to say, "We do desire so and so, because we do desire it"; and that is not an ethical proposition at all; it is a mere tautology. The whole object of Mill's book is to help us to discover what we ought to do; but, in fact, by attempting to define the meaning of this "ought", he has completely debarred himself from ever fulfilling that object; he has confined himself to telling us what we do do.[14]

13. *Principia Ethica* (Cambridge, 1948), 66-7.
14. Ibid., 73.

Mill's "simple principle", governing the right of society to legislate for morals, is flawed by the same fatal philosophical weakness. It equally falls under the crippling blows of the "naturalistic fallacy" argument. I quote Mill's principle again:

> That the only purpose for which power can be rightfully exercised over any member of a civilised community, against his will, is to prevent harm to others.[15]

The word "harm" here, like the words "pleasure/pain", "happiness/unhappiness" above, is ambiguous. It can connote physical harm or moral harm; and Mill's argument, propelled by his in-built naturalistic fallacy confusion, shifts unconsciously from the first meaning to the second and back. Indeed, the sentence which immediately follows exposes his unprotected flank. He goes on:

> His own good, either physical or moral, is not a sufficient warrant.[16]

Philosophical under-pinning so infested with logical woodworm as I believe Mill's to be does not provide a firm foundation for that philosophy of law which Wolfenden assumed and which Hart attempts to defend. This basic philosophical weakness cannot, I suggest, be ignored in evaluating Wolfenden's or Hart's reasoning and inferences.

PHYSICAL OR MORAL HARM

In fact, as Devlin has shown, the Wolfenden Committee is not consistent in its view that "there must remain a realm of private morality and immorality which is not the law's

15. *Essay On Liberty*, op. cit., 73.   16. Ibid.

business". Wolfenden says:

> We have worked with our own formulation of the function of the criminal law so far as it concerns the subjects of this enquiry. In this field, its function, as we see it, is to preserve public order and decency, to protect the citizen from what is offensive or injurious, and to provide sufficient safeguards against exploitation and corruption of others, particularly those who are specially vulnerable because they are young, weak in body or mind, inexperienced, or in a state of special physical, official or economic dependence.[17]

The Report, therefore, recommends that it should continue to be an offence "for a third party to procure or attempt to procure an act of gross indecency between male persons, whether or not the act to be procured constitutes a criminal offence", arguing:

> We do not wish to encourage the activities of third parties who might interest themselves in making arrangements for the commission of homosexual acts, even if those acts are no longer illegal. Exploitation of the weaknesses of others is as objectionable in this field as in any other, and we should not wish to seem to be countenancing anything which approximated to living on immoral earnings.[18]

It is clear from these passages that Wolfenden does not succeed, though he is often assumed to have succeeded, in making and sustaining a clear distinction between "the law's business" and "a realm of private morality and immorality". He is certainly, so it seems to me, far from succeeding in making a clean break between "law" and "virtue", or

17. *Wolfenden Report*, 13.   18. Ibid., 116.

between "crime" and "sin". In the passages I have quoted, terms such as "exploitation of the weaknesses of others", "act of gross indecency", "immoral purposes", "offensive or injurious", "exploitation and corruption of others"—all of these are, I suggest, specifically moral terms incorporated *qua moral*, into the language of the law. They have no place in the language of the law unless and insofar as the law is assuming that morality's condemnation and reprobation of certain practices is justified.

I believe that Devlin is right in maintaining that the criminal law of England not only "has from the very first concerned itself with moral principles", but continues to concern itself with moral principles. I think that he is right in arguing:

> If the criminal law were to be reformed so as to eliminate from it everything that was not designed to preserve order and decency or to protect citizens (including the protection of youth from corruption), it would overturn a fundamental principle. It would also end a number of specific crimes. Euthanasia or the killing of another at his own request, suicide, attempted suicide and suicide pacts, duelling, abortion, incest between brother and sister, are all acts which can be done in private and without offence to others and need not involve the corruption or exploitation of others. Many people think that the law on some of these subjects is in need of reform, but no one hitherto has gone so far as to suggest that they should all be left outside the criminal law as matters of private morality. They can be brought within it only as a matter of moral principle. It must be remembered also that although there is much immorality that is not punished by the law, there is none that is condoned by the law. The

law will not allow its processes to be used by those engaged in immorality of any sort. For example, a house may not be let for immoral purposes; the lease is invalid and would not be enforced. But what if what goes on inside there is a matter of private morality and not the law's business, why does the law enquire into it at all? I think it is clear that the criminal law as we know it is based upon moral principle. . . .

Other examples have been given in the literature which seem to be undeniable instances of actions or practices which have been made criminal law offences precisely because they are immoral. We have referred to the legal/moral concept of "corruption". The laws which still remain regarding obscenity are a further example.

After all, the test of obscenity given in the Obscene Publications Act of 1959, is:

> whether the tendency of the matter charged as obscenity is to deprave and corrupt those whose minds are open to such immoral influences and into whose hands a publication of this sort may fall.

There is simply no way, it seems to me, in which this language can be "de-moralised" and interpreted in an exclusively positivistically legal sense. On the corresponding United States legislation, an American judge has declared:

> (The legislature) can reasonably draw the inference that over a long period of time the indiscriminate dissemination of materials, the essential character of which is to degrade sex, will have an eroding effect on moral standards.[19]

19. Basil Mitchell, *Law, Morality and Religion in a Secular Society* (Oxford, 1970), 66-7.

Other examples can be cited. For instance, cruelty to animals has surely found its way into the criminal law because, to quote Basil Mitchell again, "we view with moral condemnation enjoyment derived from the infliction of pain upon sentient creatures".[20] Devlin refers to gambling. He quotes a Report from the 1951 Royal Commission on Betting, Lotteries and Gaming which said:

> Our concern with the ethical significance of gambling is confined to the effect which it may have on the character of the gambler as a member of society. If we were convinced that whatever the degree of gambling this effect must be harmful, we should be inclined to think that it was the duty of the state to restrict gambling to the greatest extent practicable.[21]

Similarly, the outlawing of bigamy and polygamy surely have to do, at least in part, with a moral attitude towards these practices and with a moral commitment to monogamous marriage; and it seems far-fetched and implausible to contend, as Hart does, that the intention of the law is "to protect religious feelings from offence by a public act desecrating the ceremony", and to suggest "that the bigamist is punished neither as irreligious nor as immoral but as a nuisance".[22]

LAW AS MORAL EDUCATOR

I find, once more, the root of this moral/physical, or morality/legality ambivalence already in Mill. After affir-

---

20. Ibid.   21. *The Enforcement of Morals*, op. cit., 14.
22. H.L.A. Hart, *Law, Liberty and Morality*, 41-4.

ming the absolute independence of the individual in his private conduct, Mill goes on to say:

> It is, perhaps, hardly necessary to say that this doctrine is meant to apply only to human beings in the maturity of their faculties. We are not speaking of children, or of young persons below the age which the law may fix as that of manhood or womanhood. Those who are still in a state to require being taken care of by others, must be protected against their own actions, as well as against external injury. For the same reason, we may leave out of consideration those backward states of society in which the race itself may be considered as in its nonage. The early difficulties in the way of spontaneous progress are so great, that there is seldom any choice of means for overcoming them; and a ruler full of the spirit of improvement is warranted in the use of any expedients that will attain an end, perhaps otherwise unattainable. Despotism is a legitimate mode of government in dealing with barbarians, provided the end be their improvement, and the means justified by actually effecting that end. Liberty, as a principle, has no application to any state of things anterior to the time when mankind had become capable of being improved by free and equal discussion.... But as soon as mankind have attained the capacity of being guided to their own improvement by conviction or persuasion (a period long since reached in all nations with whom we need here concern ourselves), compulsion, either in the direct form or in that of pains and penalties for non-compliants, is no longer admissible as a means to their own good, and justifiable only for the security of others.[23]

23. *On Liberty*, op. cit., 73-4.

Clearly, therefore, despite Mill's valiant efforts, in his *Utilitarianism*, to establish the principle that "society should treat all equally well", he nevertheless, in Orwell's phrase, allows some to be "more equal than others". Liberalism has never been either logically coherent enough or morally consistent enough either totally to repudiate or effectively to resist despotism—provided only that the despotic regime can claim liberal intentions, or, in Mill's own words, "provided the end be (the) improvement" of the citizens! Seventy years experience of many liberals' attitudes towards communist regimes in Eastern Europe illustrates the point.

A striking example of a measure whereby the Law set out consciously to control private morality by legal sanctions is the Race Relations Act passed in England in 1965. This Act in effect substituted "an intention to stir up hatred" for "an intention to stir up disorder". Paradoxically, it was opposed by some Conservative members on the grounds that it invoked the criminal law to enforce private morality. The "liberal" members on the Labour benches specifically argued:

> It is far better to put this bill on the Statute Book now, before social stresses and ill-will have the chance of corrupting and distorting our relationships.

Mr David Ennals explicitly claimed that the main object of the law was to shape people's moral thinking by legal sanctions.

> The main object is to change the course of events, to change human behaviour. Sometimes, one cannot change human behaviour except by having the authority to punish. . . . I should not have thought that (the freedom to stir up hatred against other groups) was the

sort of freedom that we would wish to preserve in our society.

It is somewhat unexpected to find liberals using the same kind of arguments in favour of using the law to enforce morality, for which they so vehemently criticise some judges and those whom they dub "conservatively-minded" Christians and other groups. One philosopher comments:

> What is significant is the degree to which men of radical sympathies were prepared to back legislation with a clear and primary intention of improving the ethos of our society and protecting it from corruption by racialist propaganda. Here is an issue upon which radicals (rightly) have strong feelings, as they generally do not about, e.g. obscenity, in relation to which, therefore, they employ very much the same language of reprobation as conservatives do about the dangers of pornography.[24]

I cannot but conclude, therefore, that Lord Devlin is right in claiming that *in principle* the State can legislate against immorality, and that it is not possible to fix a clear line of demarcation between "public morality" and "a realm of private morality and immorality which is not the law's business". To quote Devlin:

> If the exploitation of human weaknesses [he is referring to a phrase in the Wolfenden Report] is considered to create a special circumstance, there is virtually no field of morality which can be defined in such a way as to exclude the law. I think, therefore, that it is not possible to set theoretical limits to the power of the State to

---

24. Basil Mitchell, op. cit., 46-7.

legislate against immorality. It is not possible to settle in advance exceptions to the general rule or to define inflexibly areas of morality into which the law is in no circumstances to be allowed to enter.[25]

LAW AND "MORAL PATERNALISM"

I believe, however, that Devlin is philosophically muddled and wrong in his attempts to specify the content of his conclusion that the State can "legislate against immorality". His particular notion of "an established morality", as essential to the welfare and indeed the survival of society, seems to me to be flawed. The claims that, on the one hand, "the law must base itself on Christian morals and to the limit of its ability enforce them . . . for the compelling reason that without the help of Christian teaching the law will fail",[26] while, on the other hand, "a State which refuses to enforce Christian beliefs has lost the right to enforce Christian morals",[27] seem to me to be collectively irreconcilable and individually unacceptable.

What Devlin seems to me to be wanting to say, or at least what I suggest he ought to be wanting to say, is that the law should protect and support the fundamental human rights and the basic values of society, and those basic moral institutions which are the primary context of inter-personal relationships and which, accordingly, provide the context of moral decisions. I believe that Devlin's phrase, "the enforcement of morals", which provides the title of his book, is unfortunately chosen and is misleading about his intention and perhaps unfair to his position. Even Hart feels obliged to find a place for "legal paternalism" in his system, though he tries, with debatable success, to define it in

25. Op. cit., 12-13.   26. Ibid., 25.   27. Ibid., 5.

contrary opposition to Devlin's position and to defend it within his own legal-philosophical premises, which are ultimately utilitarian and positivistic.

THE "CONDEMN OR CONDONE" DILEMMA

Hart claims, however, that Devlin and those who agree with him make the mistake of thinking that the law is impaled on the horns of a dilemma, since they believe that the law has only two options in face of morals. They think, in other words, that if law does not condemn immorality, it *ipso facto* condones it. He quotes Lord Denning, in his speech in the House of Lords opposing the recommendations of the Wolfenden Committee:

> The trouble is that in all these cases the law must condemn or condone, and in cases such as these it must condemn; . . . it is the law alone which sets the standard.[28]

I believe that this is a false dilemma. The law can, as I believe it should, support society's moral institutions without necessarily having in each case to condemn contrary practice by imposing criminal sanctions. It is not a conservative lawyer (much less a class-conditioned judge!), but none other than Glanville Williams himself who remarks, with reference to polygamy and other "idiosyncratic" marriage customs:

> If it is thought that the law should discountenance them, this may be done sufficiently by failure to

28. H.L.A. Hart, *The Morality of the Criminal Law* (Jerusalem and Oxford, 1965), 39.

provide for them in the civil law, rather than by attempting the sterner dissuasion of penal sanctions.[29]

MORAL INSTITUTIONS AND THE IRISH CONSTITUTION

What I have just been saying has a particular relevance in the context of the Irish Constitution. Our fundamental law commits the State to legislative support of certain basic moral institutions, particularly monogamous and indissoluble marriage and the family. I shall include the texts for convenience. They occur in the chapter on "Fundamental Rights". Article 41 refers to the family as follows:

1.1° The State recognises the Family as the natural primary and fundamental unit group of Society, and as a moral institution possessing inalienable and imprescriptible rights, antecedent and superior to all positive law.

2° The State, therefore, guarantees to protect the Family in its constitution and authority, as the necessary basis of social order and as indispensable to the welfare of the Nation and the State.

3.1° The State pledges itself to guard with special care the institution of Marriage, on which the Family is founded, and to protect it against attack.

2° No law shall be enacted providing for the grant of a dissolution of marriage.

3° No person whose marriage has been dissolved under the civil law of any other State but is a

29. *Criminal Law*, cited by Mitchell, op. cit., 30.

subsisting valid marriage under the law for the time being in force within the jurisdiction of the Government and Parliament established by this Constitution shall be capable of contracting a valid marriage within that jurisdiction during the lifetime of the other party to the marriage so dissolved.

Professor Glanville Williams would doubtless be surprised and chagrined at the suggestion that Article 41.3.2° at least conforms to his own criterion that the State may "discountenance" what he might call "rational" but others with equal right could call, in his own phrase, "idiosyncratic" unions, like the remarriage of divorced persons, and may express its discountenancing of them by "failure to provide for them in the civil law".

The fundamental law of the State, with its commitment of the State "to protect the Family in its constitution and authority", "to guard with special care the institution of marriage" and "to protect it against attack", clearly has implications in terms of legislation, both as regards laws which accord with, and laws which would be in conflict with, this fundamental commitment. Much serious thinking is needed, on the part of both legal experts and moralists, as well as legislators, from their respective points of view, on these implications.

MORALS AND LAW

Radical or reformist lawyers like Professor Glanville Williams and Professor Hart, frequently reiterate that: "human law does not necessarily have to enforce the whole of morality." "It is necessary to insist on the distinction between morals and law." The Catholic moral theologian can only say that he agrees; and he can have a fruitful discussion with a lawyer starting from these premises. St Thomas Aquinas wrote:

> Human law is enacted for the community in general, and in the community the majority are not perfected in virtue. Therefore human law does not prohibit all the vices which those of special virtue avoid, but only the more serious vices, which the majority of people, with ordinary virtue, can avoid; and especially those vices which injure the common good and whose prohibition is necessary for the preservation of society.
>
> Human law aims to lead men to virtue, not all at once, but gradually. Therefore it does not require of the average imperfect man the standard of perfection attained by the virtuous; i.e. it does not prohibit everything that is sinful. If it did, the average imperfect man, unable to observe the law's requirements, might fall into complete lawlessness. . . . The laws would come to be despised and, through contempt of law, men might become more depraved than ever.[30]

No one could therefore be more emphatic than St Thomas Aquinas that civil law cannot enforce the whole of morality.

It has become commonplace to say that one cannot legislate people into virtue. There is truth in this adage, certainly to the extent that it is impossible to enforce every moral precept by law. There are many immoral actions which the law cannot and should not attempt to prohibit or to punish. There is a distinction between morality and law, between virtue and legal obligation, and between sin and criminal offence.

30. *Summa Theologiae* I-II, Q. 96, a. 2.

Distinction, however, is not equivalent to separation. It is impossible to separate law from morals or to hold that law has no role in safeguarding or promoting moral virtue. The rule of law itself depends on a moral consensus in the community. People are formed in moral virtue and also in civic responsibility by an alliance between moral conviction and legal regulation, by a combination of conscience and constraint—where, by "constraint", we mean, not physical compulsions in opposition to freedom, but that complex network of persuasions and dissuasions which society through law provides as a condition of ordered and responsible freedom in society.

Society and its laws and institutions exist because people are basically moral beings, but observation and experience (notably experience of one's own behaviour) demonstrate that we humans are prone to offend against moral values and even against our own moral convictions. One of the functions of law is to preserve the conditions and create the opportunities for people to make progress as moral beings and as responsible citizens. Law can defeat this object by being theocratic and puritanical. But law can defeat this object also by being lax and permissive. Laws which rise too far above the community's moral consensus bring the law into contempt. But equally laws which fall too far beneath the community's moral consensus, or which are an affront to the community's moral convictions, will bring both the law and the legislature into disrepute and will damage that consensus and confidence of the citizens on which government ultimately rests. We cannot legislate virtue into existence; but we can, even if unintentionally, legislate wrongdoing into existence; for we can, by legislation, create or foster conditions and trends and fashions through which the struggle for virtuous living and against wrongdoing is rendered excessively difficult.

LAW INFLUENCES MORAL ATTITUDES

It is surely undeniable that legislation has an important role in influencing or even changing moral attitudes. In countries where divorce and abortion have been legalised, moral attitudes to these issues have been radically changed, and indeed for many people they no longer are seen as moral issues at all. What is legally permissible rapidly comes to be seen as morally acceptable. Laws are, among other things, statements of what society regards as acceptable behaviour, and what is socially acceptable tends to become regarded as morally acceptable. The point is well taken in Chief Rabbi Jonathan Sacks' phrase, "the moral ecology", by which he means "that network of beliefs, relationships and virtues within which we think, act and discover meaning".[31]

An indication of the influence of law on moral attitudes is provided by recent experience of the effect of legislation on driving under the influence of alcohol. There seems little doubt but that most people have become more morally responsible in their attitudes towards "drinking and driving" since the legislation was tightened up and since the courts began to take a firm line on this abuse.

In a different context, an Irish psychologist has recently called attention to the way in which "legality and social climate are tied together". "The fact", she says, "that abortion is illegal must have its own psychological consequences. . . . Shame, guilt and fear of disapproval may reflect responses to having done something which generates social disapproval." She was talking about the consequences of the fact that abortion is illegal in Ireland, but her argument applies equally and very relevantly to the consequences of legalising abortion. The converse of her argument must equally apply: when abortion is made legal, shame and guilt

31. *The Persistence of Faith* (London, 1991).

and fear of disapproval are diminished; and this has obvious consequences for behaviour.

Indeed, arguments for legislative change are commonly interspersed with arguments for a particular moral and ethical standpoint. They belong to moral and ethical debate as much as to legal dialogue. This is often openly admitted. I have pointed out that the Race Relations Act, passed in England in 1965, and prohibiting "an intention to stir up hatred", was defended by Labour Members of Parliament precisely as being necessary in order to change human attitudes and behaviour. The law was introduced and defended specifically as a means of expressing moral disapproval of racial hatred and of expressing moral approval of racial tolerance. Similarly, the United States' laws against racial discrimination and for equal opportunities were consciously designed so as to influence moral attitudes and to change moral behaviour. In these instances, law was being explicitly invoked (and by "liberals"!) as reinforcement of morality. It is not only "conservatives" who recognise the role of laws in influencing moral attitudes. Morris Ginsberg, in a chapter entitled "Morality and the Law", in his book, *On Justice in Society*, criticises Lord Devlin for not allowing "for the part that the law may play in shaping the moral sense of the community". He goes on, in a strain surprisingly resembling Aquinas, to say:

> If the law is out of touch with the prevailing opinion, it will be brought into contempt. On the other hand, the law can do much to influence moral opinion. . . . It may well turn out that the desegregation laws (in the U.S.A.), if persistently enforced, may help to bring about a change in attitude, in behaviour and eventually in moral convictions.[32]

32. *On Justice in Society* (Harmondsworth, 1965), 234-5.

Ginsberg sums up his discussion on the relationship of law and morals thus:

> On the question how law and morals ought to be related writers on jurisprudence still differ very widely. But the view that they are independent is very obscure and I think . . . indefensible. The ultimate justification of law is that it serves moral ends . . . I know of no attempt to free law from morals which does not in the long run, consciously or unconsciously, reintroduce ethical principles.[33]

Ginsberg's views bear interesting comparison with the thinking of the Northern Ireland Standing Advisory Committee on Human Rights. In support of its recommendation in its Report for 1974-5 that legislation be introduced in Northern Ireland regarding Fair Employment, the Committee said:

> (Law) provides an unequivocal declaration of public policy . . . (and so) plays its part in effecting social change. Few in modern society would question this in the whole area of justice.

In a supposedly Christian society, people should be expected to have a well-formed Christian conscience about matters of justice in such areas as just wages, hours and conditions of work, employers' and workers' rights and obligations; about just prices, about rents and tenants' rights, about housing policy; about the problems of racial or religious discrimination; about justice and honesty in business transactions, in money and property speculation, in the

---

33. Ibid., 236.

handling of State grants and subsidies. Who would claim, however, that right moral decisions and right moral behaviour in these domains can safely be left to personal conscience; and that people can simply be trusted to be good and do good, to act justly and fairly and honestly, in these domains, without the help or the constraint of law?

A just society is one in which the laws are just, as well as the moral convictions right. Those who would assert that the State has no role or competence in the domain of conscience seem to forget the social dimension of all morality. They would themselves, and rightly, be the first to scorn the idea that we could safely dismantle the whole corpus of industrial legislation, labour relations law and social welfare legislation, and leave the domain of social justice to personal conscience, formed by the religious and spiritual exhortation of the Church and by the moral education imparted by the schools. Both of these latter are important, but they will not, by themselves alone, secure just wages, fair shares and equal opportunities, or eliminate fraud or house the homeless, or provide medical care for the poor, or uplift the under-privileged or protect the socially defenceless.

LAW AND SEXUAL MORALITY

In fact, much of the discussion about the State and "private morality" reveals an unexpected hangover of older and now discredited attitudes, which tended to identify "morality" with sexual morality. For when people say that the State must leave moral decisions to religious conviction and the judgement of conscience, it is most often precisely moral decisions in the sexual sphere they have in mind. For example, Hart remarks:

No doubt a critical morality based on the theory that all social morality had the status of divine commands or of eternal truth discovered by reason would not for obvious reasons now seem plausible. It is perhaps least plausible in relation to sexual morals, determined as these so obviously are, by variable tastes and conventions.[34]

The question which cannot be evaded here, however, is whether sexual morality is purely "private morality" or whether it has an inseparable social dimension. The moral principles involved in sexual relationships are the same as those on which public morality and indeed our concepts of the just society are based, namely: charity, justice, respect for human dignity and the rights of others, fidelity, truthfulness, respect for the solemnly and publicly pledged word. Moreover, to speak of only the fiscal implications of sexual behaviour, it is surely evident that the break-up of the family and the effects of this on children have immediate and massive consequences for the social welfare budget. The spread of sexual permissiveness and promiscuity has serious implications for public health and for the health services budget as well as for the social welfare budget. Contemporary experience surely confirms the rightness of the Irish Constitution in committing the State to legislative support of marriage and the family. Commonsense and experience show the wisdom of the State's guaranteeing "to protect the family in its constitution and authority as the necessary basis of social order and as indispensable to the welfare of the Nation and the State"; and of the State's pledging itself "to guard with special care the institution of marriage, on which the Family is founded, and to protect it against attack".

34. *Law, Liberty and Morality*, op. cit., 73.

Surely also both observation and reflection show that there are socially defenceless and emotionally vulnerable persons needing society's protection precisely in the sexual sphere. There have been few times in history, for example, when the trusting idealism of youth so much needed society's protection from cynical exploitation of their awakening sexual emotions as in today's consumerist culture, where women are depicted as universally available sexual objects; where sex itself is presented as an instantly consumable product, detached from fidelity, permanence, responsibility, or indeed love; and where there are immensely powerful commercial interests committed to exploiting sex for profit.

The enormous growth, in recent decades, in our understanding of human sexuality, has shown nothing more clearly than that sex is as much a social as a private phenomenon. Sexual behaviour is determined as much by cultural influences as by instinctual needs. In fact cultural trends and expectations create drives which are mistakenly thought to be in-built if not irresistible instinctual urges. Among the most important formative factors in the shaping of a culture or a society, are the cultural and social institutions and the legal arrangements and prescriptions which we set up to regulate sexual behaviour.

Perhaps a hasty reading of Freud, coupled with some wishful thinking, has led some of his would-be admirers to stress the "discontents" which sexual morality has brought to civilisation as if this were Freud's whole teaching: whereas his more primary stress is upon the extent to which the existence and content of civilisation have been determined precisely by restrictions upon instinctual sexual satisfaction. The time has come when Western societies have to reflect very urgently upon Freud's dictum: "Civilisation is the fruit of the renunciation of instinctual satisfaction." This is the theme of his famous book, *Civilisation and its Discontents*.

After several generations of Freudian and post-Freudian study of sexuality, some of the remarks still occasionally being made about sex as belonging to the sphere of essentially "private morality" and equating sexual freedom with the extension of liberty, can only be regarded as strangely pre-lapsarian.

Basil Mitchell, in an interesting chapter on "Paternalism and the Enforcement of Morals", in his book, *Law, Morality and Religion in a Secular Society*, follows Devlin in stressing the right of society "to protect the institutions that are judged essential to it and the morality associated with these institutions". He calls attention to the role of law in affecting the "moral atmosphere" of society. Referring to the question of "whether contraceptives should be made available freely to teenagers", he says that it can be contended

> that such action would seriously weaken an important safeguard against unwanted pregnancies, viz. the existence of a public morality condemning promiscuity.

Speaking of abortion he says:

> In the case of abortion there is a good deal of evidence that liberalising the law does not necessarily reduce the demand for illegal abortions and may even increase it, precisely because it weakens the moral restraints upon abortion.

Commenting upon Lord Devlin's point that "nonsense is made of the (abortion) law if people do not see why abortion is wrong", Mitchell says:

> But the complementary point can also be made that to relax the law very considerably would weaken the

moral restraints even further, with the result that the number of illegal abortions would continue to rise, because many more people would regard abortion as simply the long stop for contraception, and demand abortion as a remedy for inconveniences which even the more liberal law did not regard as justifying the operation.[35]

The role of civil law in shaping or altering the "moral atmosphere" of society, in supporting or eroding "public morality", is an aspect of law needing very careful study in Ireland at this time.

JURISPRUDENCE AND NATURAL LAW

There is need for a new look by law specialists and students at the Natural Law tradition as a valid, fruitful and relevant philosophical resource for jurisprudence and specifically for a discussion of the relationship between law and morals. I suspect that this tradition will have growing importance in the context of the European Community and its pressures towards so-called "normalisation" of laws throughout the member states of the Community.

Natural Law has had a "bad press" in the past decade. It is vaguely thought to be denominational, if not "sectarian", reflecting the teaching of the Catholic Church rather than this great humanist tradition. But here is one of its most celebrated statements:

> There is in fact a true law—namely, right reason—which is in accordance with nature, applies to all men, and is unchangeable and eternal. By its commands this law summons men to the performance of their duties;

35. Pages 72-3, 80-2.

by its prohibitions it restrains them from doing wrong. Its commands and prohibitions always influence good men, but are without effect on the bad. To invalidate this law by human legislation is never morally right, nor is it permissible ever to restrict its operation, and to annul it wholly is impossible. Neither the Senate nor the people can absolve us from our obligation to obey this law, and it requires no Sextus Aelius to expound and interpret it.

It will not lay down one rule at Rome and another at Athens, nor will it be one rule today and another tomorrow. But there will be one law, eternal and unchangeable, binding at all times upon all peoples; and there will be, as it were, one comnon master and ruler of men, namely God, who is the author of this law, its interpreter and its sponsor. The man who will not obey it will abandon his better self, and, in denying the true nature of a man, will thereby suffer the severest of penalties, though he has escaped all the other consequences which men call punishment.

That statement is not from a Catholic theologian or even a Christian. It is from Marcus Tullius Cicero.[36]

I believe this Natural Law to be the bulwark of all our liberties. Edmund Burke, in his speech on Conciliation with America, in 1775, declared:

> It is not what a lawyer tells me I *may* do; but what humanity, reason, and justice tell me I ought to do (that matters).

ST PATRICK AND LAW REFORM

Ancient traditions about St Patrick shed interesting light on

36. **De Republica** III 33.

the impact of the Christian Gospel upon State Law. Among the earliest legends of St Patrick is the account of his visit to the court of High King Laoghaire, at Tara. The legend seems likely to be founded on fact. According to the account, the first to stand up in the royal court and do Patrick reverence was the Druid, Dubthach, a *file* and a jurist. This account comes from the great compendium of ancient Irish law, the *Senchus Mor*. It tells of how, "after the people of Ireland had accepted the Faith from Patrick", the pre-Christian "law of nature" was combined with the Christian law, the "law of the letter", that is to say, the law of the Scriptures.

Laoghaire, however, resisted Patrick, because of the warnings of the Chief Druid, Matho Mac Umoir, who grimly foretold that Patrick would "steal from Laoghaire both the living and the dead". He would steal the living from the King by freeing the slaves and by "magnifying kins of low degree", that is to say, by abolishing the caste system. This liberation of slaves and uplifting of lower castes would extend to the next life as well as to the present life, through Patrick's "service of penance to God"; for "the Kingdom of Heaven is open before every kin of men and women having received the faith, both noble and ignoble kins; even so, the Church is open before every person of those who come under her law." This transformation of the ancient laws of Ireland by the influence of the Gospel of Christ was to be brought about "by the bright speech of the Beatus", namely the Blessed Patrick.

This account of the legal reforms which followed Ireland's conversion to the Christian faith became expanded later into a legend, according to which "a commission was set up to bring the ancient law of Ireland into harmony with Christ's law and teaching". The commission was said to consist of three kings, three bishops and three jurists. It was this commission, the story goes on, which produced the compilation of laws known as the *Senchus Mor*, which was written up for posterity in a vellum codex. It is from this latter source that is derived the ancient tradition that Patrick freed the slaves and reformed the legal system of Ireland in conformity with Christian teaching and Christian law.[37]

Two things strike me as significant about this tradition: the first is that it emphasises the power of law as transformed in the light of the Gospel to promote both freedom and justice; the second is that it emphasises the role of jurists, or what we might now call the legal profession, in bringing about this transformation. The profession of law is indeed a noble one in Christian tradition, and the law which it administers is an important instrument in the building of a community living in dignity, freedom and justice under law.

THE GOSPEL AND FREEDOM

The impression is not uncommon nowadays that liberty and Christianity are in conflict with one another, and that it is only as Church influence declines that human freedoms can flourish. A closer study of the influence of the Christian Church on the development of law would, I believe, show the opposite. The ancient Patrician tradition to which I have already referred suggests that Christian law in Ireland freed the slaves and granted equal freedoms to the lower castes. Indeed much of what is best in what we now know as the liberal tradition derives originally from the teaching of Christ, as given in the Gospels and in St Paul. Kant's great reflections upon freedom and morality derived from his study of the teaching of St Paul on the freedom with which

---

37. See Eoin Mac Neill, *St Patrick, Apostle of Ireland* (London, 1935), 101-5.

Christ has made us free. This freedom is precisely a freedom under law; for St Paul warns that we Christians "were all called to liberty"; but, "be careful", he goes on, "or this liberty will provide an occasion for self-indulgence" (cf. *Galatians* 5:13). Kant's philosophical interpretation of this Pauline teaching is that liberty and moral obligation are inseparable: "I ought implies I can."

St Paul shows how all the commandments of the Decalogue are summed up by the single commandment of love:

> If you love your fellow human beings you have carried out your obligations. All the commandments . . . are summed up in this single command: "You must love your neighbour as yourself." Love is the one thing that cannot hurt your neighbour; that is why it is the answer to every one of the commandments (cf. *Romans* 13:8-10).

The Christian commandment of love does not supersede a morality of law or a civil system of law, but it creates unlimited new possibilities for moral growth. God's infinite love and mercy and forgiveness and the absolute demands of his Kingdom, and the Gospel emphasis on conversion, repentance and the constant call to perfection, create permanent opportunities for change in personal moral direction and present an ever-present challenge to moral progress in society.

I cannot do better than end this reflection on morality and law with a passage from Pope John XXIII's great Encyclical, *Mater et Magistra*, issued in 1961 for the seventieth anniversary of *Rerum Novarum*. The good Pope John spoke of the call and duty of the Christian to work actively for the transformation of the temporal order, with its structures, institutions and laws, in harmony with the demands of God's eternal Kingdom. He wrote:

> Our sons and daughters, and particularly those of the laity, would be in error if they concluded that they would be acting prudently if they lessened their personal commitment as Christians in the affairs of the temporal order. On the contrary, we insist that they must intensify and increase it. . . .
>
> The task of the Church today is to humanize and Christianize the trends of contemporary civilization. The times themselves urge on the Church to this task. Indeed, they could be said to plead for it most urgently, not only for the sake of progress to higher levels, but even to safeguard, without undesirable consequences, that which has been achieved. As we have already said, it is to accomplish this task that the Church turns especially to the laity for their help. . . .
>
> It can be taken as certain that those human activities and institutions which are concerned with temporal affairs become better adapted for their immediate purposes when they serve also to help people's souls in their progress towards eternal happiness. The words of our divine Master are true for all time: "Make it your first care to find the Kingdom of God, and his approval, and all these things shall be yours without the asking" (*Matthew* 6:33). For the man who has become, as it were, "all daylight in the Lord" and goes about as one "native to the light" (*Ephesians* 5:8), is better able to understand what justice demands in the various spheres of human activity. This is true even in those fields in which particularly difficult problems are thrown up by individual selfishness, or by national or racial prejudice. It should be added that anyone who is animated by Christian charity cannot but love others and treat their

needs, sufferings and joys as he would their own. Aid from such a person, whatever the circumstances may be, will be steadfast, prompt, full of human fellowship and thoughtful for the good of others. "For charity is patient is kind, charity feels no envy; charity is never perverse or proud, or ever insolent; does not claim its rights, cannot be provoked, does not brood over an injury; takes no pleasure in wrong-doing, but rejoices at the victory of truth; sustains, believes, hopes, endures, to the last" (1 *Corinthians* 13:4-7). . . .

If Christians are joined in mind and soul with our most holy Redeemer, even when they are engaged in the affairs of this world, their toil will be a kind of continuation of the work of Jesus Christ himself and will thereby gain in power and merit: "if a man lives on in me, and I in him, then he will yield abundant fruit" (*John* 15:5). Work done in this way is so ennobled that it becomes a way to spiritual perfection for those who undertake it and can help to bring to others and to spread far and wide the fruits of redemption. In this way, Christian principles, like the leaven in the Gospel, will permeate the civil society in which we live and work.[38]

These words, from the Pope of the Council, point to the grave responsibilities and the great opportunities for Christian action, and particularly for Christian lay action, in today's world. Only the Gospel of Christ, lived and applied to personal behaviour and to the institutions and laws of society, can determine whether change in Ireland is to lead to social and moral betterment or is to slide steadily into decadence.

38. *Mater et Magistra*, 254, 256-7, 259.

MORALITY AND BEING HUMAN

A French Dominican entitled a lecture for the septicentennial of Aquinas: "Should a contemporary Christian moralist read St Thomas Aquinas?" Answering the question in the affirmative, Father Pohier argues that Aquinas' treatment of moral theology was highly original and that it embodies some of his best work. It might be worth adding that, in fact, the *Secunda Secundae*, treating of moral questions, is notably longer than the dogmatic-theological sections of the *Summa*. I should like, in this chapter, to advance some reasons for recommending that study of Aquinas' moral theology can illumine modern philosophy of morals, and can, indeed, point to a way of curing what, after Wittgenstein, we can call some "cramps" which affect modern ethical writing.

First of all, the very fact that we encounter in Aquinas a great mind from a culture and a philosophical tradition very different from our own, may itself help us to get a fresh look, as it were from outside, at some of our modern styles of philosophising, at their philosophical origins and presuppositions and their unargued assumptions. It needs to be recalled that every style of philosophising itself embodies philosophical postulates. It embodies, for example, postulates about what is philosophy, what is argument, even what is reason; what is fact, what is proof, what is evidence. These postulates are all of them historically situated and are in part relative to their historical situation. Seeing them from the historical and cultural "outside" can help us to see the dimension of relativity and at the same time to test the validity and truth of our present-day positions. From this "outside" viewpoint, things which seem to us today obvious may turn out to be eccentric; some of what passes for the universal consensus of all rational persons may prove to be mere "idols of the forum" or "idols of the tribe"; some of our assumed scientific superiorities may come to be seen as ethnocentric, if not insular, parochialism. Or, of course, they may not. But the experiment seems worth making; even if, as Chesterton put it, the merit of going away is the thrill of discovering home again when you return. The point is that there are many things about "home" that we never notice until we have been away and have come back. Peter Geach has said:

> The prejudices of our own period may lose their grip on us if we imaginatively enter into another period, when people's prejudices were different.

PHILOSOPHICAL "CRAMPS"

Talking of "noticing" in the context of philosophy is, of course, to recall Wittgenstein. Perhaps Wittgenstein's greatest contribution was his philosophical analysis of the nature of philosophy itself. It is banal to recall that he finds in the history of philosophy much evidence of "the bewitchment of our intelligence by means of language". He proposes as philosophy's proper task the battle against this bewitchment. Philosophers, he believes, are prone to become "bewitched", "fascinated" by one-and-only- one-true-meaning uses of words. They get caught as though with "cramp" in so espousing one of two either-or alternatives that they do not notice that the truth may be perhaps both, or perhaps neither but something else again. They become so "entangled" in reasserting the neglected side of some dichotomous dualism that they in turn neglect the alternative side. They forget that truth is more often "round" than "angular", and that "the door is round the corner". There was profundity in the casual remark attributed by someone to Wittgenstein: "The form of a philosophical answer is: 'There is the door' . . . ".

It is certainly useful to look at the history of philosophy in this light. It is revealing to consider how much of the history of philosophy has been a story of conflicts between monisms, or of swings from one to the other extreme of either-or dichotomies. How frequently philosophers have argued and still go on arguing as though one must choose one of two dichotomous alternatives: either spirit or matter; either idealism or empiricism; either ethical naturalism or ethical non-naturalism, et cetera. Philosophers often think on and think about their predecessors' thinking, rather than directly about reality. In a certain sense, as Wittgenstein saw, this tendency is inherent in thought and language itself. We are predisposed to reify abstractions, to absolutise alternatives, to be led by abstract logic to push valid ideas to irrational extremes. We are prone to follow ideas so single-mindedly that we leave reality far behind. So often, in philosophers' reasoning, facts are almost like winded empirical greyhounds trying to catch up with a metaphysical electric hare! There is indeed need to "battle against the bewitchment of our intelligence by means of language". Wittgenstein suggested ways in which this can be done; his suggested remedies are well known: "commanding a wider view"; "assembling reminders"; "noticing aspects" neglected by perhaps both participants in a polarised philosophical discussion. What I hope to suggest in this paper is that reading Aquinas can be of assistance to us in this kind of exercise in philosophical self-awareness and liberation.

PHILOSOPHY OF MAN AND PHILOSOPHY OF MORALS

Aquinas, following Aristotle, would have thought it absurd to examine ethical terms like "good", "right", "ought", "duty", without first asking questions about man, his meaning, his origin and destiny, his end. He would have held that it is impossible to determine what is good until we ask "good-for-what?"; or to determine what is man's obligation until we ask "in view of what end?" One cannot rationally enquire "What is man's good?", or "What is a good man?", until we ask, "What is man?; what does it mean to be human?" Aristotle gave central importance in ethics to the elucidation of his remarkable expression, *anthropeuesthai*, "being human". His question was: "How shall we be human?" To which question, obviously, we cannot begin to respond until we first reflect: "What does it mean to be human?"; "What manner of beings *are* we humans?" *Tines de 'Emeis*; the question has a long and distinguished history in the Greek mind. It is perhaps the central question in all philosophy, the perennial question which drives people to philosophise. The fact is, however, that it is characteristic of a long period of modern British moral philosophy that many of its trend-setting exponents were strongly prejudiced against asking this sort of question at all. For a long time many British moralists were totally out of sympathy with the Aristotelian approach to moral philosophy. H.A. Pritchard spoke for many when he confessed that he had "an extreme sense of dissatisfaction" with Aristotle's *Ethics*.

Aristotle, of course, is not the only or even the main

inspiration for Aquinas' moral philosophy. It is even arguable that Aquinas' Aristotle is not the same man as the author of the *Nicomachean Ethics*; and that the original Aristotle would not have recognised himself in the medieval and especially thomistic *Maestro di color' chi sanno*. Aquinas read Aristotle with Christian eyes and gave Aristotelean concepts a Christian dimension. From his point of view, indeed, he would have felt that the best reason for adopting Aristotle as philosophical mentor was that his concepts were capable of being given a Christian development and dimension. On the other hand, it is undeniable that Aquinas would have insisted, even if he had never read Aristotle, that the starting point of ethical enquiry must be the philosophy of human destiny, human existence, human aspiration and human striving.

By contrast, in the main stream of post-Humean British ethics, until quite recently, the philosophy of the person was conspicuously missing. The study of ethics became and largely still remains the study of ethical concepts or ethical words, ethical entities or ethical attitudes divorced from all moorings in the philosophy of the human person. There are many reasons for this. The Middle Ages tended to be contemptuously dismissed during and after the Enlightenment; although it was strange that the *epigoni* of Hume did not seem to notice how much he was himself a pupil and product of the late scholastic tradition, and how much of his *Treatise* and *Enquiry* were in fact taken up with the philosophy of the person and the psychology of the moral person. Another factor was what I think we can call the fixation with one page of Hume, the page about the irreducibility of "ought" and "is", of fact and value. This insight was treated as if it were some kind of trans-historical absolute beginning of moral-philosophical history; as though it were an unarguable first principle of all moral thinking. This page of Hume came to be treated almost as if it were the last word as well as the first, indeed virtually the only word, in moral philosophy. Again, there was the empiricist emphasis in the post-Humean tradition, involving the prejudice that whatever moral attitudes may stand for, they *cannot* be anything to do with description of facts; whatever values may be allowed to be, in no way can they be thought of as accounts of how the world is.

Less defensible still, but very pervasive, was the bias against metaphysics, and the assumption, amounting almost to a superstition, that philosophy of the person is metaphysics; and, being metaphysics, could be no fit pursuit for any philosopher aspiring to be a gentleman. The way of most British philosophers with metaphysical enquiries could be said to have been to look them squarely in the face, call them "metaphysical" in a reproving tone of voice, and pass on to a respectable topic! Some of the responsibility for this can be traced to England's brief, untypical, and unhappy experience with idealism, leading to the subsequent determination that this must not be allowed to happen again. English philosophers have certainly had a special, and in this case highly commendable, way of being ill-at-ease about moral preaching or moral edification, such as characterised many of the idealists. This was inimitably expressed by C.D. Broad when he said:

> Even a thoroughly second-rate thinker like T.H. Green, by diffusing a grateful and comfortable aroma of ethical "uplift" has probably made far more undergraduates into prigs than Sidgwick will ever make into philosophers.

These were some of the reasons why many of the central themes of the great Greek and medieval tradition of moral philosophy disappeared almost without trace from British ethical schools. As Miss Elizabeth Anscombe put it: between Plato and Aristotle and today

> philosophically there is a huge gap, at present unfillable, as far as we are concerned, which needs to be filled in by an account of human nature, human action, the type of characteristic a virtue is, and above all of human flourishing.

Aquinas, in the *Secunda Secundae* and in the moral sections of the *Summa contra Gentiles* and elsewhere presents an impressively wide panorama of the types and conditions of "human flourishing" and covers a wide spectrum of moral experience. He treats of human destiny and what the existentialists have taught us to call the "human project". Indeed, his analysis can be interestingly compared with Sartre's discussion of what he, for his part, calls man's "useless passion" to be impossibly *en-soi-pour-soi*, or with Marcel's description of man in terms of *dépassement* of problem into mystery. It is among these materials of the philosophy of the person that Aquinas finds his metaphysical grounding of the idea of the good, not as some abstract non-naturalistic attribute but as precisely the good for man, the dynamic good which motivates man's project to be a good man, in other words, to recall Aristotle's phrase, his project to be a human being, to become a human being.

Aquinas deals with human actions, which are the material of moral judgement; their freedom, its conditions and its limitations; their motivation and intentionality; the constituents of the ethical context which situates them and which conditions the application of general moral principles to a concrete moral situation. He deals extensively with the psychology of choice and with what we would now call the psycho-pathology of choice, in other words, to use the modern jargon, with "liberty-in-situation".

Aquinas devotes several long chapters to a detailed examination of virtues and vices, their psychological basis, their bearing on human excellence or human flourishing, their embodiment in human actions and their contribution to the making of good or bad men and women. It may be remembered in passing that since, though not including, Hume, almost no main-stream British moral philosopher has included in his ethical studies either virtues or vices, or at least not until the past decade. Aquinas deals thoroughly with law, divine, moral, civil; with divine and natural law as the basis of moral obligation. He presents moral law as the ultimate basis of that community consensus about the good life and the good society which civil law presupposes; although civil law, of its nature, in part goes beyond and in important part falls short of what morality requires. Obviously, also, Aquinas is characteristically concerned with that transvaluation of moral values which is brought about by the New Law of Christ.

This is only a very schematic outline of the scope of Aquinas' moral thinking. It is clearly a wide sweep. It would be absurd to claim that he has "all the answers". There has been a manifest explosion of knowledge and enlargement of experience since his time, which he could not have even foreseen. There has been considerable methodological gain derived from the demarcation of disciplines and from specialisation in all domains of learning; and all of these have brought genuine progress. Nevertheless, I would claim that modern moral philosophy, and particularly in the British tradition, has been the poorer, not only in range but also often in depth, because of its ignorance of many of the thomistic insights and its narrowing of the scope of moral philosophy as compared with medieval treatments. There has been a narrowing of vision; there has been a restriction of the range of moral language; and this, I suggest, has produced certain typically Wittgensteinian symptoms, "cramps", pseudo-problems and even mistakes.

I propose to select two areas of modern moral discourse in an effort to illustrate my point. I am going to suggest that the ground could be cleared for progress by an attempt, in Wittgenstein's words, to "broaden our horizon, seek out other pertinent examples, so as to 'command a clear view' of the range of the language of morals". Specifically, I want to suggest that Aquinas could be of assistance in just this attempt.

If I might be allowed to be facetious for a moment, I could suggest that sometimes an Irish bull has more philosophical meat than a charollais—or a cartesian—one! Here is one which perhaps has a message for philosophers: The tourist, according to the story, asks a local resident: "How do I get from here to Roscommon?" The answer is: "To tell you nothing but the truth sir, if I was going to Roscommon, I wouldn't start from here." There is a serious point to this story in this context. Philosophers sometimes do get lost because they start from the wrong place. What moral philosophy then needs is a new starting point.

WHAT IS GOOD?

The place from which most of the main-stream British moral philosophy has habitually started is that page from Hume's *Treatise*, to which I have already referred; that page which every schoolboy, or at least undergraduate, used to know almost by heart:

Take any action allowed to be vicious, wilful murder,

for instance, examine it in all lights and see if you can find that matter of fact or real existence which you call vice. In whatever way you take it, you find only certain passions, motives, volitions and thoughts. There is no other matter of fact in the case. The vice entirely escapes you, as long as you consider the object. You never can find it, till you turn your reflection into your own breast and find a sentiment of disapprobation, which arises in you towards the action. Here is the matter of fact; but 'tis the object of feeling, not reason. It lies in yourself, not in the object. So that when you pronounce any action or character to be vicious you mean nothing but that, from the constitution of your nature, you have a feeling or sentiment of blame from the contemplation of it.[1]

It seems a pity that British philosophers have not applied to this page their anti-metaphysical reflex. For this is precisely a page, not of empirical observation, but of dogmatic metaphysics, no less dogmatic and no less metaphysics because it is empiricist metaphysics. But alas, when one is thinking within a tradition it is very difficult not to regard its unargued assumptions as self-evidences; instead of which they may be prejudices.

A.J. Ayer, in a paper entitled, "On the Analysis of Moral Judgement", reproduced this passage in his own words, although his words were almost a verbatim reproduction of the words of Hume. Ayer clearly regarded the statement as, in effect, self-evident. He speaks of "the police-court details" of an alleged crime; and he holds that these contain no item which could conceivably count as the "moral wrongness" of the crime.

1. Hume, *Treatise of Human Nature* (Oxford, 1949), pp. 648-9.

This separation of fact from value runs through most modern British moral philosophy. It is, I believe, an error, and an error with particular unfortunate consequences. British schools of moral philosophy may differ, even differ fundamentally, on many matters. They may—secularly speaking—excommunicate and anathematise one another as objectivist to subjectivist, non-naturalist to naturalist, et cetera; but they almost all agree on separating value from fact, moral *ought* from objective *is*; they nearly all regard moral description as a non-factual assessment, whether it be non-natural or emotive; or else as a personal decision, the adopting of an attitude or the recommending of a decision, the taking of a stand or the making of something "my policy".

The whole thing, I believe, involves a confusion. Only empiricist philosophical "cramp" could have led the normally cheerful Scot to suppose that the "passions, motives, volitions and thoughts" involved in "wilful murder" were the "facts" of the murder and were in themselves morally neutral and distinct from the "vice" of the murder.

THE WRONGNESS IN WRONG

Another moral philosopher (Bernard Mayo), spoke of the difference between the factual-historical statement, "Hitler persecuted the Jews", and the moral statement "Hitler was wrong to persecute the Jews". The former, the factual-historical statement, is, he holds, decidable on the basis of facts about which all must agree; while the latter, the moral statement, is not similarly decidable and is not susceptible of universal agreement. Now this is surely a glaring instance of a good philosopher's flying in the face of reason and reality because he has been mesmerized by a theory. I submit that we are just as sure of the objective wrongness of the Holocaust as we are of the historical facts. Consensus is as possible in the one case as in the other. Dissent from the moral judgment is just as objectively mistaken as it would be from the factual statement. Indeed dissent in the moral case is as objectively erroneous as it is morally reprehensible. What, after all, *is* wilful murder except an action or the bringing to be of a state of affairs characterised by morally wrongful "passions, motives, volitions and thoughts"? The immorality of the murder is not a further fact (whether a "non-natural" fact "in the world", or an "attitude-fact" in the observer); the immorality is *in* the facts described, because precisely they are not "neutral facts" but ethical facts, the adequate objective description of which necessarily includes their evaluation.

It becomes plausible to treat the "facts" of a wilful murder as ethically neutral only if we, on the one hand, define "facts" as the referents of scientific descriptions; and, on the other, regard moral judgements as the expression of some kind of non-rational and emotionally-coloured personal attitudes. The "facts" of a wilful murder are indeed "ethically neutral" for a psychiatrist, a criminologist, a social-statistician, et cetera. But that is because such specialists as these, in the interests of particular scientific tasks, have *abstracted from* the ethical content of the facts. The morality of a situation is indeed what the sciences omit from their descriptions; but this is by no means to say that the morality is non-factual, in the sense of being non-objective or merely attitudinal.

Philosophers seem to become so mesmerised by the science-model of a "fact" that they can produce lists of obviously ethical predicates, yet blandly and without any sense of incongruity describe these as "neutral" and as still requiring to receive their ethical content from elsewhere, namely from the attitude of the speaker. One American moralist, for example, Mr Paul Edwards, held that a certain wicked American senator's "deliberate distortion of facts, his spite and desire for revenge" are non-ethical predicates; and that to call them "evil" is to "add a definite indication of the speaker's attitude". A British colleague, Mr Montefiore, proposed to regard the description of someone as "truthful, dependable, helpful, affectionate", not as a moral evaluation of that person, but as factual reasons justifying a moral commendation of him. These seem to me to be instances of the philosophical malady diagnosed by Wittgenstein, whereby intelligence becomes "bewitched by means of language". These are instances of a similar fallacy as that which led Ayer, in *Language, Truth and Logic*, into the impasse of emotivism. Ayer managed then to convince himself, and tried to persuade his readers, that "stealing" is a merely descriptive, ethically neutral word; and that the note of "wrongness" is communicated to it by the tone of horror in which I say it or by the exclamation marks which I add when I write it.

THE EGOCENTRIC PREDICAMENT IN ETHICS

Related to this fallacy is the further fallacy of supposing that moral evaluations are necessarily personal and subjective and therefore cannot claim objective or universal validity, since by definition they are someone's evaluations and cannot be independent of that someone's thoughts or feelings or language. This, however, is a rather familiar fallacy. Paradoxically, it is a fallacy which any British philosopher would immediately recognise in the field of theory of knowledge. It is in fact the solipsistic fallacy, or the egocentric predicament, which philosophers in the Humean tradition have long delighted in exposing as the root fallacy of idealism. I have referred to this fallacy earlier, dealing with a section of the Wolfenden Report and other examples (see pp. 11-13 above). Happily, after Wittgenstein, it is now a commonplace to say that sentences of the form, "I know that . . .", "I believe that . . .", do *not* refer to my thoughts or feelings or inner states of mind, but to objective facts.

The egocentric predicament has often occurred in the history of ethics; but, very strangely, in this field the very same diagnosticians seem unable to recognise the very same symptoms. But it is precisely the same fallacy. It is this fallacy which led some egoistic hedonists to deny the possibility of altruism, on the grounds that, if I desire to be unselfish, then unselfishness is simply a desire of mine; and any desire of self is tautologically a selfish desire! In other words, unselfishness would turn out to be merely my peculiar brand of selfishness. Here, for once, the idealists devastatingly had the right of it. It was for this sort of ethical fallacy that F.H. Bradley reserved his most withering scorn:

> That I do what I do is an idle proposition. That it should lead to a new result would be strange, unless truth were to be found in the barest tautologies. . . . "I know what I know," "I experience what I experience," "I want what I want"; indeed here be truths; but it is a poor neighbourhood where such truths can be considered as making the fortune of a philosopher.

Let us take such a statement as: "Deliberately to torture a human being is intrinsically and absolutely, everywhere and always evil." This statement is, in one sense, dependent on my thinking it and saying it. But to say this is to say something utterly trivial and quite literally of no philosophical or moral consequence. Such a judgement cannot be thought without someone's thinking it; it could not exist as a statement without someone's stating it. But, in the only meaningful and important sense, what is being asserted by the statement is being asserted as a truth, independent of my or anyone else's thinking it or saying it. What is being claimed by the making of this statement is that the *truth* of the statement does not depend upon "anyone's thoughts or feelings or language". And this claim cannot be refuted by saying that the judgement is "somebody's value judgement".

THE NARROWING OF MORAL VOCABULARY

The confusion about value as being non-objective, non-factual and non-universalisable has other sources also and has yet wider ramifications. It vividly illustrates the fatal consequences of narrowing the range of moral language so that the narrow list of words allowed to be "properly moral" are cut off from their existential hinterland and their anchorage in reality and are thereby deprived of real moral content. If only such terms as "ought" or "right" or "morally good" are allowed to be "properly moral terms" or to express moral judgements, then all possible descriptions of states of affairs and all possible accounts of what people do are condemned to be non-moral; and then the moral evaluation of states of affairs and of the deeds men do is left to be imported into the state of affairs or into the account of the activity from outside the situation by the judging subject.

Miss Elizabeth Anscombe, whose insights so frequently recall to me the insights of Aquinas, delivered a celebrated and, at the time, highly controversial broadcast, "Does Oxford Moral Philosophy corrupt youth?" In it and in subsequent writing, Miss Anscombe finds the theory of rootless "oughtness" to be the cause of most of the muddle and error in British moral philosophy since Hume. Her argument, as I see it, runs that, as the term "morally ought" is used by many modern moral philosophers, it supposes that an action, over and above the complete factual description of it, must have some additional, special, moral (and therefore non-factual) quality before we can call it "morally wrong" (or right). This is why we can have such follies as Mr Mayo's looking for reasons to prove that it was "wrong" for Hitler to persecute the Jews. It is almost as though "moral wrongness" were something else than plain "wrongness" and had to be specially proved over and above "ordinary wrongness". This is why Miss Anscombe bluntly urges that, in the interests of clarity and precision of thinking, the words "morally wrong" et cetera should be provisionally banished from ethical discussion. She declares:

> It would be a great improvement if, instead of "morally wrong", one always named a genus such as "untruthful", "unchaste", "unjust". We should no longer ask whether doing something was "wrong", passing directly from some description of an action to this notion; we should ask whether, e.g., it was unjust; and the answer would sometimes be clear at once.

But how can you do this if you define moral philosophy as the study of moral words, and if you confine moral vocabulary to a restricted range of "properly moral words"? How can you evade such fallacies as those indicated above if you leave out of moral philosophy the whole area and the whole language of passions, emotions, dispositions, habits, virtues, vices, and all the other multiple and varied ex- periences and realities which formed the main content of such moral treatises as those found in Aquinas and other philosophers in the Greek and medieval tradition? It is precisely such analyses which constitute the descriptions that call for and that justify the use of moral words and the enunciation of moral judgements. For all these are descriptions of human reality; but they are at one and the same time moral descriptions.

Happily, however, there have been many indications recently that these deficiencies are being detected and are gradually being remedied. The same Bernard Mayo wrote a book, *Ethics and the Moral Life*; and the very title in itself indicated a very significant change in the climate in British moral philosophy. Stuart Hampshire, in such books as *Thought and Action*, asked questions which British philosophers had scarcely thought meaningful for centuries; such questions as, "What constitutes being a good man?", a question to be answered in terms of "the distinctive powers of humanity". More unprecedentedly still, he then wrote:

> The only critical ethics is a story of ideals of human excellence that at the same time points the way to the future of these ideals.

The writings of Alisdair Macintyre take much further this new and exciting departure in British moral philosophy, and siqnificantly he acknowledges indebtedness to Aquinas in his work.

CONSEQUENTIALISM

The term "consequentialism" is again a term I borrow from Miss Anscombe. It is the term she uses for what she holds to be the error common to almost all English academic moral philosophers since Sidgwick. They have, she holds, put out a philosophy according to which, e.g., it is not possible to hold that it cannot be right to kill the innocent as a means to any end whatsoever and that someone who thinks otherwise is in error.... Now this is a significant thing: for it means that all these philosophies are quite incompatible with the Hebrew- Christian ethic. For it has been characteristic of that ethic to teach that there are certain things forbidden whatever *consequences* threaten, such as: choosing to kill the innocent for any purpose, however good; vicarious punishment; treachery . . . ; idolatry; sodomy; adultery; making a false profession of faith. The prohibition of certain things simply in virtue of their description as such-and-such identifiable kinds of action, regardless of any further consequences, is certainly not the whole of the Hebrew-Christian ethic; but it is a noteworthy feature of it; and if every academic philosopher since Sidgwick has written in such a way as to exclude this ethic, it would argue a certain provinciality of mind not to see this incompatibility as the most important fact about these philosophers, and the differences between them as somewhat trifling by comparison.

This paragraph is a quotation from Miss Anscombe's article, "Modern Moral Philosophy", in *Philosophy* (January, 1958). She concluded that article with these words:

It is left to modern moral philosophy . . . to construct systems according to which the man who says, "We need such-and-such, and will only get it this way", *may* be a virtuous character: that is to say, it is left open to debate whether such a procedure as the judicial punishment of the innocent may not in some circumstances be the "right" one to adopt; and though the present

Oxford moral philosophers would accord a man *permission* to "make it his principle" not to do such a thing, they teach a philosophy according to which the particular consequences of such an action *could* "morally" be taken into account by a man who was debating what to do; and if they were such as to conflict with his "ends", it might be a step in his moral education to frame a moral principle under which he "managed" . . . to bring the action; or it might be a new "decision of principle" making which was an advance in the formation of his moral thinking, to decide: in such and such circumstances one ought to procure the judicial condemnation of the innocent. And that is my complaint.

These have been long quotations. They are, I believe, justified; because I know of no better statement of what really is *the* issue, not only in contemporary moral philosophy, but in contemporary society. I contend that it is also the distinctive contrast between almost all contemporary moral philosophy and the moral teaching of Aquinas. I believe that it is here, more than anywhere else, that contemporary moral philosophy both can be constructively criticised and needs to be corrected by insights inspired by Aquinas.

The issue, however, is not just an academic one. I believe that the fundamental issue in morals and in society today is the question: "Are there actions which are absolutely wrong in themselves, so that it could never be morally right to do them for any reason?" Most contemporary moral philosophers, at least as far as their theory goes, agree that there are no such actions. Very regrettably, some theologians have come to hold similar views.

But the doctrine of consequentialism is very widespread

in modern society. I suggest that we see it translated from theory into abominable practice in the physical and moral ruins we have witnessed in the North of Ireland over the past couple of decades. The doctrine of consequentialism is, when we do get down to street level, that morality which holds that the end justifies the means. What is it but the belief that morality comes from intentions and not from the intrinsic nature of acts that has led to the claim that murder, mutilation, or "punishment shootings", the use of "proxy bombs", intimidation, destruction of property, robbery, protection rackets, depend for their morality on whether or not they are perpetrated for "the Cause". This malady of morals is not, however, even in practice, confined to the terrorists. Paradoxically, one has to conclude that it is the same sort of belief which has, for example, led eminent legal authority to declare formally that "physical ill-treatment" is not "brutality or cruelty", unless there is a "disposition to inflict suffering coupled with indifference to or pleasure in the victim's pain."[2]

I suggest that a legal judgment such as this—and it is, in my view, a morally and ethically disastrous judgment—could never have been handed down unless generations of academics had been conditioned by a moral philosophy which maintained that morality is to do with the agent's feelings, attitudes, emotions, in other words states of the mind, rather than with what one actually does, what change one actually effects in objective reality. The result is a morality whereby it is intentions and motives which alone determine moral distinctions; and the end, whether it be "Security" or "the Cause", can justify any means, however evil such means might be in themselves, or however evil

2. See the Compton *Report of Enquiry into allegations against the security forces of physical brutality in Northern Ireland arising out of the events of 9th August 1971*; H.M.S.O., Command 4823 (November 1971).

they might be granted even by their agents to be for other people in other circumstances, or even for themselves in different circumstances. The philosophers who worked and taught in the tradition I have been discussing would themselves, I know, have abominated and utterly repudiated such a morality in practice. They did not foresee and would not even concede that such conclusions could follow from their theorising. And yet, I contend, a moral philosophy of "consequentialism" must lead, and has led, to such results as these, and can be invoked to provide sophisticated and plausible justification for such results. Pascal was right when he said that "to think rightly is the first of all moral duties".

The future of our society, indeed the future of humanity, may well depend on whether we can restore the conviction that some actions are evil in themselves, no matter what "loving" motives or what noble causes or what honourable or "tolerant" intentions or what desirable consequences may be alleged to follow from them and no matter how learned or how "compassionate" are the legal or medical specialists who carry out or who approve them and no matter what Constitution or what law may permit them. No "noble" revolutionary or security motives or "good" political or social consequences will ever justify such actions as murder, torture, kidnapping, robbery, protection rackets, extortion, drug-dealing, planting timed bombs in aircraft, deliberate bombing of civilians in war, taking or killing of hostages. No cause or end or intention or motive will ever justify religious or racial discrimination, religious persecution, genetic engineering, "ethnic cleansing", sectarian killing. No profit motive or pleasure principle will ever turn pornography or prostitution into acceptable businesses. No European community law or bureaucratic decision will ever make abortion a morally acceptable "service". Torture is still torture even when it is deemed necessary for "taking terror by the throat". Racial discrimination and apartheid are still evil when, and perhaps particularly, when designed to preserve white "civilisation". No claim for "progressive" or "non-judgmental" attitudes will ever turn sodomy, adultery, promiscuity, paedophilia into moral right or human rights or even into meaningful sexual freedom. The question as to whether there are actions which are in themselves intrinsically and absolutely and always morally wrong is a fundamental area of disagreement between much modern moral philosophy and even some modern moral theology and Aquinas. I believe that not just Catholic moral teaching but reason and common sense tell us that Aquinas is right. The question is of importance for moral philosophy. It is of vital importance for the future of humanity.

RELIGION AND MORALITY

Another virtually unargued assumption of the prevalent contemporary moral philosophy is that ethical relativism is the morally superior attitude. "Absolutist" ethics, such as religious, metaphysical, and, in particular, Christian ethics is very widely held today to be uncritical, conformist, intolerant, fanatical, reactionary, extremist, fundamentalist. Miss Iris Murdoch speaks for many when she expresses the fear that "moral degeneration through lack of reflection" will result from metaphysical or absolutist views of ethics. Linguistic moral philosophers, existentialists, positivists, as well as marxists and neo-marxists and paradoxically many liberals, all agree in this kind of assumption. It is this which places most contemporary moral philosophy in its most striking contrast with the moral teaching of Aquinas.

The view could be said to pass for dogma in moral philosophy today that belief in absolute moral truths or in intrinsic and immutable moral principles entails intolerance, fanaticism, smugness and hypocrisy, opposition to moral and social progress, resistance to "liberalising" legislation. A typical expression of this may be found in the following paragraph from Stuart Hampshire:

> For a man following a code of explicit and exhaustive instructions, moral issues would be matters of casuistry. He would be the type of a fanatic, because only certain already listed features of any situation would be worthy of serious thought before action. He would be governed by words, fitting words to facts, as lawyers must.

The adherent of a religious moral code, Hampshire continues, is in this danger. He may feel that he is "following explicit instructions which he believes to be God's instruction". His code may seem to him to be an "established morality that is already complete".

Such a man, he contended, has no place left for "morality as exploratory thinking, as an unresting awareness of that which he is neglecting in his intentions". Intellectually and morally satisfied with his code, sanctimoniously satisfied with himself, such a man has

> a morality without perpetual regret, because it is without any sense of a morality left to itself. . . . Intellectually and philosophically, it often rests on a naive confidence in established classifications of specific situations, actions and mental processes as being the permanently obvious and self-justifying classifications.

Such a morality is, almost by definition, "abstract", "unreflecting", "sheltered". We are by now prepared for the magic word which British philosophers since Karl Popper have borrowed from Bergson, but have not seemed to realise that they are using in a sense precisely opposite to that of Bergson: an absolute morality is a "closed morality". Contrasted with it is the "critical morality" of "changing ideals"; the historically-progressive morality of "open and always disputable" concepts.

The Christian will certainly be puzzled to find his or her understanding of the Christian ethic included in this description of "closed morality". A Christian philosopher will be likely to recall that Bergson himself, who first introduced the terms "closed" and "open" morality, applied the latter term specifically to the Judaeo-Christian ethic; for he saw in it, and particularly in the teaching of Jesus Christ, that call to the never-ending, never-finished pursuit of moral perfection which for Bergson precisely defines the "open morality". Let us consider, for example, the Ten Comnandments, the Sermon on the Mount, or Christ's own "new commandment", "Thou shalt love thy neighbour as thyself. . . . Love one another as I have loved you." Or take the parable of the Good Samaritan, or the sentence of the Judge at the Last Judgement: "as long as you did not give . . . (food and drink, housing and clothing, nursing and respect and love) . . . to one of the least of these my brothers or sisters, you did not do it to me either." How could anyone seriously claim that to live by an absolute moral code such as this is to confine oneself to "only certain already listed features of any situation"? How could anyone assert that such a morality as this can be lived out by routine or conformity, unthinkingly and unreflectingly? What plausibility can there be in the suggestion that one is "sheltered" by it from "unresting awareness" of one's moral unworthiness, from "perpetual regret" and repentance? Surely such a morality as this, if really believed to be absolute, can never be a "morality left to itself", or will ever afford us justification for complacency, will ever give us respite or simply leave us in peace? Richard Hare once spoke disparagingly of those for whom "good" . . . means simply "doing what it says in the Sermon on the Mount". But surely when he wrote that he could not have been actually thinking about "what it says in the Sermon on the Mount". He goes on to remark that such people "act always by the book". If we substitute "New Testament" for "book", we shall see at once how thoughtless and careless a thing it was that Mr Hare said.

I refrain from developing further here the dimension of depth and seriousness which religion brings to ethics, and from drawing further upon Aquinas in illustration of this dimension. At least this, however, could surely be asserted without much fear of contradiction: namely that it would be naive to think that one could remove religion from ethics, and leave ethics unchanged. Surely it would be disingenuous to suppose that one could exclude religious questions from philosophy and leave philosophy unchanged. If the human being is a religious questioner, then to exclude religious questions from the philosophy of the human being is to postulate an utterly different philosophy of being human, that is to say to postulate a different species of man and woman. Religious questions, I submit, are questions that define human nature. To cease to ask these questions would be to set arbitrary limits to the question with which we began, the question which defines both the philosophy of morals and inseparably the philosophy of the person, the question: "What is the meaning of *anthropeuesthai*?"; "What does it mean to be human, and what kinds of actions are becoming to a human being?" "What does it mean to be human, and how does one become a good human being?"

Nietzsche summed up morality in the phrase: "Become what you are." We could translate this as: "Become human." The term "human" has a moral meaning as well as a descriptive one. This is shown in the use of such moral terms as "humane", "humaneness", "humanity", "inhumanity". The human being is the only being whose existence is as such a moral project, a being whose mere existence implies duties and rights. It is not simply that he or she is human; he or she *becomes* human by actions "becoming" to the human being. To discern and identify what those actions are is the business of moral philosophy. To make those actions our practice and our habit is for each of us our personal moral project, our way of being morally good by being fully human.

FORGIVENESS

I leave to the end what is most distinctive and indeed unique in Christian morality, namely the dimension of repentance and forgiveness. Christian moral teaching, as outlined above, insists on the absoluteness of moral law: certain acts are absolutely and intrinsically, universally and always, wrong in themselves, irrespective of motives, intentions or consequences, and other acts are right in themselves.

But this teaching is not a prescription for unhealthy guilt or self-loathing. It is instead an invitation to repentance, an occasion for conversion and a promise of forgiveness. These are the central emphases of the teaching of Jesus Christ. Discussion of them is almost completely absent from modern moral philosophy.

The public ministry of Jesus begins and ends with the call to repentance and the offer of forgiveness. Jesus began his preaching with the words:

> Repent, for the Kingdom of heaven is close at hand (*Matthew* 4:17)

Repent and believe the Good News (*Mark* 1:15).

Jesus' last instruction to his disciples has the words:

> So you see how it is written that the Christ would suffer and on the third day rise from the dead and that in his name repentance and the forgiveness of sins would be preached to all the nations (Luke 24:47).

When one thinks of what "being human" would be like without the sense of needing forgiveness and the hope of receiving forgiveness, without the readiness to forgive and the humility to accept forgiveness, one can better appreciate the extent to which Christian teaching brings about a "transvaluation of all values", transforms moral philosophy and enlarges and elevates our understanding of "being human". Contemporary humanism is a pale and emaciated creature without the Christian dimension.

One philosopher who grappled with these questions was Aquinas; and both his questions and his answers can be relevant to our questioning today. It was no accident that, just as he held philosophy, the work of reason, to be *semper perfectibile*, so he held humanity and each human being to be *semper perfectibilis*. He not only believed this and taught this; he tried personally to live it. Not content with being a philosopher, he strove to be a saint. That was his way of being fully human. Like St Ireneus, he believed that "the glory of God is the human being fully alive," having life and having it to the full.